SLANG*ETRY

(The EDITED Verses)

Po·et·ry [pṓ .uh. tree] 1. Literary works ; verse writing of high quality, great beauty, emotional sincerity or intensity, or profound insight

Slang [slang] 1. Very casual speech or writing: words, expressions, and usages that are usually considered unsuitable for formal contexts

Slang*etry [slang. uh .tree] 1. A combination of slang and poetry, with the verbs twisted the way only T.T. King can   2. A thought inducing serum of inked verses to stimulate emotions i.e. extreme laughter, intense tears, wistfulness, joy …

SLANG*ETRY

Slang*etry is the definition of life
broke down to it's simplest
With some tears mixed in the ink ... for emphasis
Mama and dad, told me not to elaborate so much
But, I get all emotional
and sometimes things just need to be said
the way they need to be said
And if I can't find a microphone that reaches around the globe
- then this thing is just gone have to be read
By all the chicks like me, who people agree won't ever get ahead
Because we got soft behinds and hard heads
and all we wanna do is ... dream
I wrote this for my belief in the One who promised me
that in Him I can do all things
and I wrote this for my - way too skinny girls
And for those of you who 'think' you're way too fat
If you like eating your Doritos girl - it's somebody out there who would sell a small part of
his soul just to buy you a snack
And I wrote this to all my 'living in the hood' girls, who commit crimes
'Cause your flower bloomed from a vine that was entwined in that hood- life grime
You grew thorns around your petals to protect what was sweet inside
and to keep from losing your mind
'cause ambulance sirens were your lullabies...
the devil rocked you to sleep some nights
and you got slapped whenever you cried
you might turn into – and this goes out to :
all my grown women doing jail time
and the good girls reading this to occupy your mind
Because, you can't find a good man to date
... and you refuse to settle so , your morals always seem to get in the way
To all you party chicks that date way too many

Drink too much and get way too friendly
For all my broke chicks, who are just reading this
because, you ain't got no phone minutes
to all y'all spoiled girls who got everything plenty
Y'all business chicks that cut checks & verbally slit necks
To my sistahs living in the streets
who don't know where your next meal is at
God has an angel out there for you Girl, believe that
To the deceitful girls that get all you can scheme
you're just missing that one thing ....
maybe it's just the right man's touch
And to all of you who crave the touch of a woman- some would say way too much
To all the new hoes - and the old pros
For all Y'all sexy flirty over thirties - and the young swinging singles
To all my widows
To y'all crying and staring out window's
Slang*etry is personal conversation between me and every chick who ever read it
And every man who get a chance to see it
Because, it's poetry about us - the ones they love
The joy bringers ... the keepers of trust
Wouldn't be a single thing in this man's world if it wasn't for us
This book of slang is a national women's anthem
slash/ survival manual
keep it around for when you need it
I expect every woman in the world to buy my book and read it
.... then pass it around and repeat it
Because, I wrote it for all of y'all
but just as much for me ...
like therapy

Slang*etry

Nikki You Were So Beautiful

Nikki you were so beautiful ..... you had big lips and they were your real lips
You had long black hair down to your hips
- and it was your real hair
and Nikki, you stayed up on the real truth
Until, you ran up on a lie
With that 'fresh out of jail' smell
He was always talking about his convictions
- and what a hard life he'd been through
Impassioned speeches about how all he needed in his life ... was you
To complete his change
.... and 'keep him straight'
To us - that man was see through
 But, you accepted every color he showed you
You took every blow he throwed you
because, he was like a preacher to you
accept he taught you things you couldn't learn in Sunday school
Made you the main link in his chain of fools
.... and there were obvious signs of abuse
Because, there's only so much Maybelline can do
But, under every bruise
You were still cool
You had a smile every time I saw you
Plenty of laughs every time you rolled through
- and you were beautiful Nikki
You were so beautiful ....
To him - his hands around your throat was a method of control
To you - it became a love hold
To me - a wolf devouring a dove
- was the only way to describe y'alls love
The deeper he sunk his teeth in
The more you asked me to stay out of it
 ... So, I did and I watched you laugh through busted lips
and wanted to have his throat slit
- to be around to help you deal with it
But, I had cried my last tear for you ...

I just prayed every day that a change would come through
Plus, he kept you on your knees
so, you were closer to God than me
But, it was plain to see - that you were so beautiful, Nikki
Even when his TKO's
Put you in ICU
He had pushed away your family so, I cried over you
Under all the black and blue and the feeding tubes
You were still beautiful ...
And invincible ... indispensable
Because, when I looked at you in that bed
You weren't you - you were the old 'us'
You were age thirteen in a park swing
Feet dangling in the dirt as we discussed things
Like the boys we wanted to kiss ...
and who was whose boyfriend Micheal Jackson or Prince
With our New Edition t-shirts painted on
Remember? I had the blue - and you had the pink one ?
I remember how we used to laugh - until we cried
And how we cried - when all we could do was cry
Until we were purified
... like when my brother died
And you basically moved in with us because, you refused to leave my side
You kept saying that he was an angel now, so everything was gonna be alright
The darkest hour of my short life girl, and you were the light
So bright ... and beautiful Nikki
... you were so beautiful
And when you finally did get out of that hospital bed
He sent you right back in an ambulance
For telling him that you knew
That he got the HIV he gave you, from another dude...
- yet Nikki, you were so beautiful
...'that with some of the last words from your lips
You told me to forgive
And with your last breath ... you reminded me to live
Because, silly me, I never believed that you could ever die ...
Because, I was always the wild one - and you always did right
- I never thought I'd pick up the phone and you wouldn't be there for me to call ....

or that your beauty would become so painful I'd take your picture off my walls
And box up your beautiful smile ..... crying all the while
"Nikki, you were so beautiful ...."
Because, the world lost space after losing you
The reason it all happened, only God could have knew
since you were a flower child
We buried you in the moonlight
I swear, all the roses bowed down when your casket passed by
The sky opened up and the angels cried
The Weeping Willows shed real tears ... and the earth sighed
- the world stopped spinning cause your beauty had died
Or maybe ... it just seemed that way to me ...
Because my eyes were guided by misery
So, if you're listening to this poem and you could be Nikki
Imagine your best friend is me
Writing poetry you'll never get to read
Trying to make some peace with your tragedy
Because, if you're anything like Nikki - then we all agree
..... that you're beautiful
And Nikki -whatever star you are when I look in the sky
With my heart calling out and my eyes searching high
You're beautiful
Nikki, you're still so beautiful ......

DEDICATED TO :

Those who have lost their lives for what they thought was love
– no matter what the name, place ,date or race
And to you - if you're in a domestic situation, please remember all of the loved ones that you will leave behind for the
hate – wrapped love of one person.
There's always an angel out there, sometimes they come to you
... sometimes you have to go look for them –Seek Help
We all know the slogan, "Love shouldn't hurt."
that's true... *

PLEASE DON'T LEAVE ME (A Ghetto Love Ballad)
PART I

Please don't leave me
Baby ... please don't go
If you walk out that door
I'm gonna make sure everybody knows that
- you take those blue pills
- That Benz is rented wheels & you're just a boy still
'cause, your grandma pay's your cell bill
And if you *do* leave - just make sure that you know
that my love ain't no revolving door
once you leave, you can't come back no more
I know you're angry now
- and baby I accept that
This one is all my fault , I'm sorry - I admit that
But, we've been invested since our first kiss
We decided on forever, when we started - so we can't let it end like this
 and this isn't the first time our thin line between love and hate has been argued
 down to non - existent
We fight with every word - heart blows that we know will inflict the most hurt
and when that doesn't work -we use our fists
– usually with me throwing the first lick
and breaking the windows out of your whips
and snatching tracks out of the weaves of any chick you dare cheat on me with
one second we're locked in death grips in front of the kids
the next we're clenched in our favorite ghetto kiss
because, that's just how our love is ...
and how many times have we done this
- for you to be saying that this time – that this is really it?
... and we've been connected at the soul for so long... that I can feel it
'cause through everything - I never would have believed I would see this day
 where I would rather go blind- in that old Etta James moan and writhe type way
than to be standing here watching you trying to walk away
though, we both have to change if you stay
we can't keep having a different version of the same fight every day
and you can't keep trying to throw us away over simple thing's
Especially, after all the times that I've stood by you

I've been your alibi – more than a few times
 - lied to the Feds for you *and* went to jail for you
Every time you were the one locked up -
I was the one who made your sales for you and hustled up your bail for you
I did a lot of things, that I hope don't come back around on me - just to keep a roof over our bed for you
I've never once asked for a ring to signify me
just allow you to declare me and deduce me to 'Wifey'
 and, have literally been here in sickness and health for you
Every single time you've ever been sick
      Who picked up and fixed your meds for you ?
 and before you could even speak the words
      Who locked & twisted every single dred on your head for you?
The <u>first</u> time I held a gun while we were on the run
      I vowed 'til death do us part' for you
and after all these things I've done
    I'm sitting here having to beg for *you ?!*
You need some time alone ?
I respect that
but, when you say you're *leaving*
- I reject that
And I know you're about to ask- that if you're so bad
- then why am I trying to keep you?
It's just the simple fact – that no matter what you lack - I still need you
And more than that , I need to complete you
I need to stay this thing on your arm that makes other men wanna be you
I need to keep loving you for exactly what you are – and nourishing your potential
Plus- no matter where we are your arms are where I still feel most protected
And the man I know and love wouldn't just leave me out here lonely & neglected
So, baby please, go put those bags back .... relax and unpack
Oh - you being hardheaded ?
Well, I take every one of my words back:
Boy - don't let the door hit you
Where the good Lord split you
 you need to call Tyrone to pick you up off my porch
 And here boy - take your kids with you
Now, don't get me wrong
I know I'm gonna miss you

But for now - don't worry about forgetting my face
 I'm texting you a deuce picture
and a message about how
 - I'm through with you
You're so stuck in this dumb stuff - that ain't nothing else I can do with you
because, I'm on some grown woman
two thousand and twelve bizness
& if you can't deal with it
Be free to go get some lame chick
Somehow, you just don't get it
So, yeah, boy let's forget it
- That's all you dismissed
You're going to be the one who regret's this
Now get your fingers out my door -
Before you get your hand squished

PART II (A GHETTO LOVE BALLAD)

I watch all the drama right here where I always sit
or looking, like this through my blind slits
I gotta watch everything out here, because it's definitely watching me
It'll be the same ghetto drama next Friday & Saturday
If it ain't these two fighting again - it'll be Lisa and Randy in 3G
when Lisa find's out that Randy got another baby on the way - in building E
because, ain't nothing new under the sun ...
if you done heard one ghetto love ballad –you've heard all of 'em
Love ballads 'round here - are wrote in dark chords - about court dates for child support - and paternity...
- The lyrics are about cheating, lies, gambling, addictions, lost hope and ghetto dreams
- drama queens, drug fiends and deadbeats
 - little ghetto superstars whose light may never reach maturity
love tragedies, emotional catastrophe's & the constant vibratos of arguing
echoing through the walls & the concrete ...
everybody singing their part - to the same tune with the notes gone wrong
on life's broke down piano ,with most of the keys long gone
Just hear it ...
Waking and sleeping to it until, the tune gets engrained in your spirit
The rich folks - that ain't dope fiends - can't stand to hear it because, they fear it

They lock the sound behind bars, so they don't have to be near it
or try to kill it
- because it's old Cocktail walking the same streets every day
 - her hips chiming they wares ... advertising her pain for sale
crescendo of the baby's screaming, the ones who need they comfort and the ones who will never receive it - so eventually, turn into these little beasts that roam the streets
- because they learned not to need it
It's the sound of little girls lullabying in they childish, grown woman soprano's – for the boys and the men to come & get it if they want it ....
 Lulling their big heads right to sleep and waking up the little heads that don't think ...
The girl with the least amount of clothes on will probably be pregnant by the end of the week
That's usually how all these babies 'round here adding up statistically from what I see ...
Then there's the tambourine of bicycle pedal squeaks - only the crack head's riding
I remember the days when we could innocently play all day , before they even had street lights
 Now the kids have to stay inside because it's too dangerous in the streets
their new toys are cell phones & t.v.'s
the ringing and videos add to the melody of
 basketball dribbling, sweat dripping like water
 dope boy's hollin' that they got it
I take my drink outside, after I get my cigarette lighted
Because, I heard handcuff jangles blending in like a violins
'dem blue boyz out here picking up Pee Wee again -
Bass baritone for me to call his mama and 'them ...
     - I probably won't do it though –
I hope they keep him locked up this time
         - 'cause lately he been running round here doing his usual
He's always somewhere around the scene whenever something gets stole
- and he's supplying all these kid's around here with this dope
'because he's the rap lyric underneath the ghetto - Telling these little saggy pants boys how a little money can restore all they lost hope, how:
 "If you got to sing the blues surrounded by poverty – you ain't got to do it broke, just do a little bit of work for me and go buy you some shoes and a new coat, get your swagger up ...", I done heard him rap them lines a million times, and them little boys always dance ....
 so, I let his is acapella get drowned out by the sirens
 and the fighting,
 and the crying

and the violence
and the blood that sings out from the grass , when you walk over where somebody died
though most of them lived in vain and died at a young age
... they don't wanna be forgotten
- drum taps of all the footsteps that keep on walking
Domino clackers
- choruses of laughter -
Singing 'Ooh', altogether because, Brenda just brought home the new triplets , after having three miscarriages in two years - and we harmonizing in ghetto ballad unity about- "Oh how sweet God is, because whatever He takes - if you keep faith , He replenishes .With Brenda singing the loudest Amen
- on top of the tap, tap of Sister Black's heels on her way to evening service with them grandkids, praying all the way, for they mama ('cause ain't no telling where that girl is)
 - on top of the alto wail of Chanel downstairs because she done got fired again
– on top of gossip
- on top of liquor swills & huffs of whatever type of smoke
until, it all swirls together into one note
that you're lucky if you ever heard
        - and blessed if you haven't
- if you ain't got issues with my ghetto you welcome to come by and share it ....
ain't no solo's here but if you want a part on the stage you can have it
& our attention, if you can grab it
While we create our own singing roles and do our own vocals
        - in our GHETTO LOVE BALLAD...

I SCREAMED

I screamed one night
Because no one heard my whispers
I screamed because I had lost my voice
The voice that said – I am somebody
I screamed because the world had told me
That my words didn't matter
I screamed until my lungs hurt
I screamed because my heart hurt
I screamed because it wasn't fair
That no one cared - that I screamed
I screamed that night because
There was nothing else that I could say
I screamed for all the things
- that I didn't have and I never would
I screamed for all the times I was hurt
... and had remained silent
I screamed so loud that I scared myself
I screamed because, I *was* scared
I screamed so loud that it shook my soul
I let that scream take control
I screamed so long and hard from the pain
That it sounded like thunder trapped in rain
The night I screamed

NIGGA

(A Love Letter To Black Men)

Baby, I don't call you NIGGA lightly
- I call you NIGGA
because, it might be
That thing that can flip that mental switch
and make you regress into your black consciousness
- take some of the air out of your arrogance
and make you re-visit a day you never even lived in
when black wasn't just the color on your skin
- It was the part of the bus you sat in
It was 'Colored Only' drinking fountains
It was your forefathers who couldn't read or write
But, marched all night, hefting signs that read 'I AM A MAN'
And real men like Medgar Evers, who died so you would
never- ever have to be called ,'NIGGA' again...
And since NIGGAs was such a beautiful thing back then
The trickle-down effect is that - if we were friends
I would call you 'My NIGGA' as a term of endearment
But, for you I mean NIGGA in its ugliest sense
Because when you talk to me NIGGA - you don't make no sense
You got kids you made NIGGA - and ain't spoke on since
You chase me like a dog that has caught my scent
And even though I'm your reflection you call me a bi***
- So, what does that make you NIGGA ?
And plus, you spit lines like a bad rap lyric on repeat
That's why I can't be bothered to speak
Because, I'm looking past you for a real NIGGA
A swagger even when he's standing still NIGGA
An educate my mind and keep it real NIGGA

A touch me deep- inside my soul somewhere .... so, I can feel NIGGA
- that can look me in my eyes and not just at my behind as I pass by
- unlike you NIGGA
And I would give you some clues on some thangs you could do to work on you - but you're
too impressed with your fake jewels
and your whack homeboy crew
and bragging about how all of your baby's mama's just love to stalk you
and not getting dirt on your tennis shoes
Which- was- made –to- walk -in -dirt
- didn't nobody tell you, NIGGA ?
And I feel bad that you so dumb but, it's got you by this long
I just wish I could reach around all the hoods and take all your little boys
into my arms
- so they don't grow up to be like you NIGGA
But, I still need to see your beauty in the world's big picture
Now, I might cuss you out - if that's what I have to do
And I might hate a lot of your ways but, I will FOREVER-
FOREVER LOVE YOU
... N**GA

Today I Smiled

I smiled because I realized that my
circumstances

do not outweigh my possibilities

I smiled because I understand that

God is the only power in my life

I smiled because I know that whenever

a door is closed in my life

God's eyes are always on me and

Heaven is open for eternity

I smiled because I have my health

I smiled because although my children are the greatest test of my strength

They also give me the strength to go on

I smiled because my daughters smile is so beautiful

I smiled because when I look into her face - which is her father's face

I see her absolute beauty and not his mistakes

I smiled because my son has inherited all of my best attributes

- and made them better

I smiled because I know that I can turn my obstacles into opportunities

I smiled because I have the knowledge to pray

I smiled because I only have five dollars in my pocket

-because yesterday there were none

I smiled because even when I have no place to go

I have the ability to...

I Wanna Spit

Spit [spit] - *slang verb* (used without object)
1. To say, speak, talk
2. To sing or rap
3. To eject from the mouth ; to throw out like saliva
4. To set a flame to
(i.e. what a superb lyricist can do to a mic)
- Slang*etry definition
1. To speak from the heart about a subject of vast importance
2. What I wanna do right now :

I WANNA SPIT until - I don't wanna cry no more

I wanna spit until there is NO SUCH THING AS WAR - I wanna spit to get away from the soldiers cry's ... and my own "Lord why's".

I wanna spit until I change history and misery/ poverty / incestry/ child molesting/the music industry and a government that spins the truth into make believe... I wanna spit until I've tear drenched faces and made changes

- I wanna spit until, every word in the dictionary falls out of my breath

and I can't say anything else

– I wanna spit the world open and introduce myself

-I wanna spit until the last word stated leaves space vacated and souls medicated

- I wanna spit so hard that I feel touched by God -

I want to spit until time re-arranges and BRINGS OUR HEROES back, spit the mothers off crack - spit this load off my back - spit our souls back on track

- I wanna spit little pregnant girls' stomach's - back flat ... and if I can never spit like that -
I'll spit enough so that they will know that a bulging belly is only a bump in the road - another hand to hold - a chance to mine gold

but, I wanna spit the daddy's back through the doors un-ashamed ,un-shackled and un-blamed. Because, I'mo spit 'em back changed and mind re-arranged, integrity reclaimed, understanding ingrained, they're going to be soul saved and black history trained ... so their smiles don't feel strange to children who never knew their names ...

- I wanna spit back open the church doors - spit until I find that one endless sentence with just the right words. I wanna spit to say what I mean and mean what I say, I wanna spit me and my family into some brighter days.

And I wanna spit about my kids because their names are etched into my skin, in ink of Indian and the love is born in - I wanna spit until, *they* don't wanna cry no more - I wanna spit until *they're* free- Because, the same things I spit for myself

– I want to spit for them until my last breath

- I want to spit cause they carry mama's name

- and carry mama's thangs

and kiss mama into sweet dreams -

- I wanna spit him into the next Martin Luther King

and spit her until she can earn her own rings and buy her own things

- I wanna spit until they understand that that there is a Father on high who will never leave-

so high He sees their every need,will never leave

promised in His word that He would never deceive

– He will never need a reprieve

and He's only as far away as their knees...

- I wanna spit until there's always presents on birthdays

- Spit this soul flow until I can't think of a- single soul thing else to say

- Because when I think about my last few pennies spent

- my due rent- these last and evil days and this economy predicament..

- I WANNA SPIT

UGLY POETRY

I write ugly poetry – because, it's the truth
Ugly poetry – because, it's about you
Ugly poetry – because, besides my face
ain't nothing about me cute
Ugly words – because, ain't nothing else I can do
Because, life gives me an ugly attitude
I steal away & write poetry in the backpacks of runaways
To document they last days
I sit in the black bile
- In the hearts of pedophiles
And write ugly poetry-in ugly tears
whenever they touch a child
I write ugly poetry on metal
slung out barrels by the devil
Ugly poetry across my t.v. screen
When I look at BET
because, those video girls don't reflect me
Those studio molds don't impress me
So, I write ugly poems about the industry
Because, the mediocrity distresses me
Then I take my pen and write in dark ink
on dirty sheets - where HIV leaked
For those positively tested ... 'INFECTED'
.... for everyone who's been raped or molested
For little girls that leave their wombs unprotected
For every child in the world that's neglected
Because, all I write about is what I see
and when I look around me it's all ... UGLY POETRY

Mama

When my legs were just a

thought in my father's reality

Mama, you carried me

When I saw my first hint of the sun

Mama, you were the ray of light

When I didn't know arms

I knew your embrace

On your breast I found my security

My serenity, my identity

In your smile, God answered the question that I knew not how to ask

They rejoiced the squeal of a newborn child

Only you knew the meaning

You heard me call your name ...

Mama ...

A Single Mama's Prayer

When everything's falling apart, Lord
Let me keep it together
& remember to praise you every time I see
the sky - no matter what the weather
Send your Holy Ghost & your angel's down -
to guide us through this day
& give us peace when we pray
Let us sleep ... sweet when we lay
& Lord, Please - help me to raise these kids
Bless their natural father wherever he is
and whatever he has chosen to do
If he refuses to know his children
Please Lord, Let Him Know You
Let me be a woman in every way
& become more like you every day
Let my words drip like honey
& my names like fine ointment
Let my destiny be - more than I can dream
- Because, you appointed it -In the same tone -
as when you said "Let There Be Light"- and the sun shone
And Lord, please forgive me for all of the wrongs that I've done
Let this prayer come to you pure as I kneel at your throne
& Lord, please keep me ... and give my family
.... a portion of your blessings
I am so longing for your favor ... let some drops fall on me
Let me be the best mother that I can be
Let me not bow down to sin -
Because these kids look up to me
Give me wisdom when I speak
And let me practice what I preach
Make my kisses extra sweet
Lord, bless the work of these hands &
Let me walk with love, grace, joy and intelligence
If you could, Father, send on that good man
- Amen

 Invisible Butterfly

Always in someone else's sky
U fly through so many springs
On those delicate wings
That catch air and flutter
With their translucent colors
Those other exotic things
That float haughtily when the wind breathes
Don't have the wings that you grew
... or love the flowers like you do
Such a pretty little butterfly
Can't wait 'til I reach my eyes
And see your rise
On wings that grew so strong that they split the sky
and aerodynamic so they death defy
- so beautiful that they mesmerize
Because, though it seems that no one else can see
You are, it's clear to me
The loveliest butterfly in season
If for no other reason
While you flew through the noons
Than that you broke from your cocoon

I'M A WHINO (SO WHAT ?)

I consume mass quantities of liquor to clear my mind yo'

Straight out the bottle like a whino

If you don't like it don't mind me because, I'm fine yo'

- and quit talking that mess about rehab – Because, I said No

'Cause , see – I drink with specific intent

To circumvent all the madness and the idiots

To combat all the sadness and the stress fits

Waiting to tell the landlord that I don't have all his rent -

Because my check ain't even cashed and it's been spent

But , I do have four dollars .. and a few cents

So, so what if I wanna kick it with my best friend Gin ?

Fall in the bottle she's wrapped in until we both trapped in

And I'm drunk again ...

You gotta atone for your own wrongs

So, can't mines just be my own bizness.. ?

So what if I go into a trance, drop my pants and do a handstand ?

Black out in church – Hike up my skirt and give a lap dance ?

I'm the life of the party

Teach you how to be naughty

-Make you glad that you met me

AND I'LL DRINK WHEN I'M READY ...

I WON'T EAT 'TIL U LOVE ME AGAIN

I won't eat 'til U love me ... again
I'm going to lay in the middle - of this empty hole in my soul
And caress your picture ....
I'll let my lips fade away ...
If I can't kiss you .....
I will refuse to speak
If I can't say, I love you and your name
..... in the same phrase to your face ...
Because, I need you
Like the air
needs the wind .... to breath
like a greedy man .... need's everything
So, not even a morsel will cross my teeth
Until, I waste away ...
I swear in a blood oath - signed this day
That I won't eat until U love me .... again

CHAMELEON

A CHAMELEON is a no good man
with a little finesse
He knows how to make you feel sexy
- when you know you look a mess
He tell's you he love's what you got on
no matter how you're dressed
... he's a chameleon
He blends right into your skin
From the outside in
So carefully his colors keep changing
The Chameleon
Uses his lips like a paintbrush until the hues set in
Until the two of you are one shade completely blended
He builds you sandcastles in the sky
Built from whatever dreams & sweet things you like
The chameleon has that steady sincere stare
when he tells you how much he cares
He's gonna give you everything you want somehow
... he just can't get it for you right now
'Cause the only green in his pocket is weed
The good kind, with no seeds
That's why he ain't got no money to take you out to eat
Doesn't matter 'cause he's already blended in
Y'all melded into one person when he first touched your skin
... and he keeps you so fed emotionally
You don't care if you ever eat again, personally
Because, y'all like all the same songs
and he introduced you to some new ones
And one chameleon has replaced ALL of your best friends
Because, they don't have his arms to wrap you in
& keep complaining about what kind of shape y'all in
while the chameleon
understands you and keeps you laughing
tells you to stay home with him instead

and lay around in bed
And the chameleon - is skilled at blending onto your couch
When you start to fuss - he just blends his tongue into your mouth until you
forget what you were mad about
Resumes his video game after he's thoroughly
worked your body out
steadily those colors change every day
in different shades
The best colors fade away from his array
until only his darkest colors are on display
for you .....
and then you realize that his color changes are becoming mutual when he's
blue - you are too
- though your shade is more true
'Cause he's his own worst enemy so, you're always trying to protect him
He's always down and out- so you're always trying to help him
When he's yellow – the two of you are ecstatic together
You make magic together
and your smile is bouncing off his skin ...
Your yellow is because he's telling you, that you're beautiful again
His yellow - is because the compliments got you to do something for him & you
always gotta have him
So you gotta move him in
'Cause when he's gone you can't stand
...the blackness of his absence
Now you green cause chicks calling his cell phone
Then red again because yo' anger gets him turned on
Then black & blue, cause it's you he put's his hands on
Then clear when he's gone 'cause that's the only color that tears come..
So, you pray until the sky turns yellow and the sun turns blue that he'll come back
home
Cause' when the Chameleon leaves -
all your colors are gone ...

You Make Me Miserable

Cupid shot his arrow in me
he must be blind and can't see
That you make me miserable
You shouldn't be nobody's first love
because, you make me miserable
and pitiful
You're selfish, deceitful and wrong
... but parts of you are beautiful
And the bad thing is that you know
.... that you make me miserable
You make me miserable because your lips are so sweet
Sometimes they're all I can eat ...
'Cause I was broke down on the side of my life's road starving for love
when you found me
and coaxed me ... until you finally got your arms around me
My heart got full off the lies you fed *me* because I was so ... hungry
phase one in your diabolical plan to forever own me
and oh ... your misrepresentations tasted so sweet as they were going down
in your ... slow deliberate doses
Because, I was just as cautious - as I was lonely
So, we can both agree, that you tricked me
into melting into this puddle at your feet
& now that, your puddle my position currently
- you keep trying to drown me emotionally
You keep the water deep with these tears you continually make me weep
Thick and murky with your, aforementioned, lies and deceit
You make me so miserable some days
that I wish you was a stomach ache
So, I could just throw up all our memories
... and flush this love away
along with the sweet things - the man you used to be .... used to say
that keeps me stuck with the stranger you've become - every day

demanding the woman in me to love him in all my old ways
and this fickle chick succumbs to your old kiss ... and obeys
Because, that phony still uses your voice when he says my name ...
that animal ,guttural ,beautiful ,haunting ,wanting sound that my soul always
re-plays ... Like a song whose words you forgot,
that only I still sing
When you're making me miserable, I hum the refrain
Because, all I still wanna do is dance through life with you
holding me the way you used to ....
I say we make some type of exquisite manure
out of all the crap we go through
which is considerable
I probably won't ever stop loving you though
... even though
U MAKE ME MISERABLE

CUPID

I try to blend into thin air - So, Cupid won't notice that I'm here
I'm tired of ducking & dodging him
Because, Cupid is my worst enemy
I find him to be juvenile, hostile and unfriendly
He's always shooting poison tipped arrows at me
He keeps my heart panic caught , shell shocked
and paranoid because, he won't stop
He's the reason I can't even write no love poems
& slap me if you ever hear me sing a love song
Because, when I find Mr. Right - Cupid turns him wrong
He play's mind games with trillions all day long
and he still won't leave me alone because, Cupid is stupid like that
He'll put the man I want in my path
Then before I can get him in my grasp
He'll put him right next to a prettier girl - then shoot him real fast
and laugh - Then bring me something wack and burnt black
And shoot me in the back
Sometimes, he'll bait a trap for me
with some sexy thing - A man that fit's me perfectly
Somebody who loves the fact that I'm complicated, and will do anything to be with me
Have me daydreaming about wedding rings
and then he'll blow away in the breeze
Because, Cupid loaded up a trick arrow & only shot me, obviously
From Anthony and Cleopatra - to Adam and Eve
To the last person I dated - and me
He's been waging affection wars throughout history
So, he's better trained at love combat than me
So, when his arrows kill my heart finally
He resuscitates me ...Then sends his friend Lonely to asphyxiate me
Until, I feel like if somebody don't hold me properly
I will literally cease to breathe ...
I wish Cupid would just let me be ...
But, for some reason he always wanna mess wit' me...

Call Me

I just wanted to tell y'all this one I wrote one night .... about one of my old love's
.... because he was on my mind at the time
I remember that boy used to have my heart singing all off key like ...

I can't get you out my mind
I think about you all the time
Why don't you call me ?
Don't you wanna call me ?
Please won't you call me ?

Then I would just drown in the silence of my phone without his ring
then when my cravings really took control
I would call his number then hang up the phone
He would see my nickname scrawled across his caller id
then he would press send ... and he would call me
and he'd be like 'Hey girl , where you been ?"
..... like he had been looking for me
 and just the sound of his voice would make my knees go weak
So, even though my mind would disagree
.... my lips would scream
Sitting here melting ... waiting for you to come jump in ....
and he would say he was coming over .... and that when he got by my house
...... he was gone call me
Then he would come over with that look
 - that he knew would melt me all over
he would ... say all the little words he knew would help him get over
he would ... kiss me in the spots he knew he owned ... all over
- then take his little pieces of me and disappear - all over
I'm talking about - that boy had me laying down the history for Usher songs because I had it bad I was stuck in the house
I don't wanna have fun –because that boy was all I was thinking about
Until, one day I got tired of his stuff
All I could have was his body and that wasn't enough
I deserved more than his spare sex and his rare texts
After he put it down all around town - I got what was left

I knew he wouldn't ever love me

at the same time - I remembered how much I loved myself

and Daddy always told me I was a queen

therefore it was furthermore behavior unseemly

and absolutely beneath me

to be treated as anything less

So, I left a note on the door

In big block letters that he couldn't ignore

It said : IF YOU LOOKING FOR A GOOD TIME THEN BYPASS ME CAUSE THERE'S A BRAND NEW WOMAN SLEEPING IN THIS BED AND AIN'T NO VACANCIES . NOW I APPRECIATE ALL THE LITTLE THANGS THAT YOU BOUGHT ME AND ALL THE LESSONS THAT YOU TAUGHT ME , LIKE THE FACT THAT I CAN'T LIVE WITH YOU KILLING ME SOFTLY , SO BACK UP OFF MY PORCH AND UP OFF ME !

So, the next time he saw me – his eyes picked me out the throng

I had my baddest jeans on and my hips was singing a new song

that went :

'Hey don't you like that ?

Tell me don't you miss that ?

Wish you could come back

But baby don't call me.'....

DRUNK TEXTING (again)

I deleted your number for self - preservation
To negate my proclivities for drunken textation
with poetry about missing your lips
and your fingertips & telling you how much I wanna touch you ..... I found myself
drunk texting you at the club
and on the bus - Sipping vodka all day getting messed up
Trying not to think about us
Not about our history because there wasn't that much
Because, we was over before we even got started
Which is why I be texting you like I'm retarded
Because I'm tipsy & I can't barely see
36858863 for "do you (still) love me?"
When I know you never did
I just remember times when we used to kiss in the dark
two zippers apart
And start daydreaming about having your kids
and start drunk texting again
Thinking up schemes to get next to you
& dat Vodka be hollering "Girl, you know what to do
Text him and see if he's thinking about you too ..."
That's why ... I erased your number
So, I'd quit waiting for your ringtone to wake me up out my slumber
Talking about some," *Boy I need you bad as my heartbeat, bad like the food I eat, bad as the air I breathe...*"

Some lady don't even know brainwashing me
To the point where - you couldn't even wake me up
Because, thinking about you- I can't sleep
& we was only together a few weeks
But, it was strange
Because, everywhere I looked I saw your name
Like the elements was telling me u was supposed to be my man
And the funny thing, is that *I let u* go because I saw your game
At first, I put on my poker face
And tried to bluff you into thinking I was real sophisticated and slick
The type of woman you needed to be with
hoping your opinion, of what I could be to you would switch
After you dropped that big secret about your main chick
& I realized you were being slick
So, she could get all the good gifts and I'd be your on the side thang
That chick that has no name
Which dictates that in the natural order of these kinds of things
- she gets the wedding vows and the sweet nothings
I get stuck trying make our nothing into something
But, if only for one last time - I wanna have your lips on my cheek again-
and chugging down this Vodka, I'm a mess again
I'm trying to remember your number ..... so I can text you again

Candy Had A Problem

Candy had a lot of problems- she would do anything
or any drug she could obtain
Looking for something or someone that could solve them
Cause' candy's main problem was her self
She would rather go out and hustle – than ask for help
Her head was a brick wall - with 'I ain't listening' graffiti' d on
& Candy took every step on her road of life anticipating a fall
Because that girl was scared of her greatness
Scared of being alone
Scared nobody would love her with the lights on
She was scared of everything
And scared of nothing
Cause 'Candy, deep down, was fearless ...
She was angry with all men
Yet, she craved their nearness
Because, they were validation to her,
... that she was somebody
She didn't even know 10 times 10
She dropped out of school so her real education could begin
But she could estimate every baller by the size of his rims - She could calculate how to get
herself next to him - Then be in the same negative situation all over again
Cause' candy had a problem
Her problem was her mama who didn't treat her with no interest
So, she used her body like an atm trying to get riches
So she could stunt in front of her home girls - in her new expensive, labeled stitches
You couldn't hear the name Candy without hearing, 'Mayne, you gotta show her the
money first - after that anything goes ' ...
Because, ' Candy's main life goal - was being bigger & better than her heroes - which were
video hoes and chicks that swung around on stripper poles - Making that flossy, drift
through they fingers type dough - that would eventually drift up their nose - in white
dopes.. Candy saw it every day and still refused to know, that she was the same little girl,
that they were ... blowing through life out of control ...
just looking for daddy ... or like Candy - a product of his unusual sex ...
She was loud and wild so she stayed surrounded by men that didn't show her no respect

Because, the only word they knew how to call her - was b****

Anybody who ever told her they loved her - was tricks

So ... a person could understand her problems

I stood around with her one day trying to help her solve them   -

But her mind was too re -arranged for me

Candy said, "I stand around in broad daylight and darkness is all I see

You tell me there's a God on high -but , ain't got no proof for me - Ain't no God that I can see-& no way you can make me believe

That a Being up in a word as sweet as Heaven, would pave these dirty streets

And make this type of life - for me to have to lead

' she looked so sad when she said to me ... ' Un uh ,' ain't no God in this place "...

And I wanted Candy to know that only a creator with the mastery of angels

- could have created something as perfectly exquisite as her face ....

So, I asked her , "Well, - what other way could u have come to

Be - from a microscopic piece of jelly?"

She said, "A donation from a man who wasn't nothing -

A contribution to my mama's belly ... in exchange for something - either money – or

whatever she was smoking at the time

... The tears in her eyes belied her shoulder shrug,

making my arms pull her into a soft hug on their own accord.

I could see that Candy needed to see a lot of things,

the main thing I could show her was some love

.... But she couldn't connect with the feeling , so she pushed me away with a look that

killed me - then went with her speech:

"Why you standing here trying to act like you care about me?

You just like the preacher man and the missionaries that wanna pray for me for free

but, wouldn't give me a spare dime for something to eat.

And I got business to do so –

I'm gonna have to ask you to get away from me."

I looked at her and wished I had a whole' 'nother lifetime to try and tell her all the things I learned growing up

-& that when she was down in the dirt , all she had to do was look up-& to place her value
further than what was under her mini-skirt
but , I never got the chance
by the time I got my words together
- Candy was at the wrong place - with the wrong man,
bullets killing both her and the target intended
- The newspaper would read , 'Only Seventeen
- A short Lived Legacy - Life Ended'
- I heard 'the hood' robbed her of all the clothes and jewels she was so attached to
- and even took her shoes before the paramedics could zip her away in a disposable tomb
But, I also heard , from good witnesses ... that she had a cross clutched in her hand ...
So I can only hope that Candy made it on high
and He - reached her before me ....
Finally gave Candy some peace
...and absolved her of all her problems ....

I NEVER

I never finished anything but high school
And two stomach terms
I made it to 34 years but, only finished 23
My immaturity is a negative
So, I have to take a few years back
I never finished loving nobody
Or being kissed right
Or learning how to love
.... properly ... Or telling mama
How much I appreciate her
Or telling the world my stories
- so, still I write ....
I never finished changing anything
That matters yet
So, every day I try to change myself ....
I never finished my whole bottle
So, I take a little sip every day
I never finished raising my flowers
Sometimes ... they wither at my touch
Even though I love them so much ...
So, I water them with secret tears
And ask God to bring sunshine
I never finished laughing
So, I dig for joy
In the dark places my mind goes
I never finished the perfect poem
But, I will when I finish achieving
I never finished praying
& I won't as long as I'm breathing
I never finished crying
Because, tears will always be
Blessed to us since mother Eve
To purge until we're free
I never finished trying
I refuse until, I cease

I LOVE YOU

I love you so much that I wrote I love you
+ plus your name
+ plus mine ... a trillion times ...
Until, the words blurred together and spelled = FOREVER
... then, I buried the pages under a rosebush in a soft rain
and kissed all the petals until night came
and under every kiss, I whispered
– I love you, because it's true ...
I love you in a way that could only be described by Eve,
when Adam gave his rib so that she could breathe.
But, you gave me your entire heart without a thought.
So ... that's why I love – you ... As, I lay quietly under the night sky, no one asks me
why, they know it has something to do with my love for you ...
As cupid's smile accepts my skin under the shooting stars,
I wish I love you's to you again and again, while I watch them fall
Because, I love you so much that it seeps from my skin
like passion fruit in one of Heavens gardens.
So, that the un-loved breathe our essence
...and believe in God ...
I love you so much
that it hurts my heart just to feel your touch
But, that's okay.
Some people would give anything to feel this sweet a pain,
just one time ...
to be loved in kind
.... the way
I LOVE YOU

DeadBeat Poetry

I'm writing deadbeat poetry on the child support papers
My calm hand, doesn't waiver
I'm writing my soul flow all across your name
Hoping to never see it again
And page after page
I'm writing the sourness of this document into lemonade
And making this bitterness sweet ...
I've acquired a taste for the drink
If it were up to you
It'd be a nasty brew - ain't that true?
I'm writing over the words of what you're putting me through
In dark black ink, unaffected by you
But, nourished by the inspiration
of such an ugly situation
As you and the things you do
And the turmoil you put our child through
With your careless attitude
You'd rather stay wrong, than even try at doing good
As customary – You unrepentant and contrary
You got thousand dollar speakers, that pump hits of idiots -
Screaming 'Baby mama's ain't nothing
- on top of a bass beat and random cussing -
But, what is a deadbeat that inspires poetry and
Collaborates in ho-etry ?
Lives to deceive
And doesn't care where his child
... breathes or what he plans to achieve?
U don't have an idea where he lays his head
if he's being fed
he could be dead
While you're lost off in your own world
spreading your seeds to the next girl
When I think about - a person who don't get it

You're who the description fits ... to me
..... You should feed your mind on this
- baby-mama-ology the logic that gives me this peace
While you go out of your way to initiate emotional brawls
And try to leave me with scars
... so go ahead baby- hit me one more time
the pleasure is all mine
because, I'm still going to stand strong
- hold on tight to this baby and move on
Because, I know about your own scars
That run way deeper than ours ....
some of them - I put there myself
And something else - It's evident
From the time you've spent
Wreaking havoc on me for this child to see
That what came from my womb
Will never love you ....
because, now anytime his thoughts on you have to be explained
- he uses your first name
Though, he probably does yearn for you
Just hates the things you do
- And you could be the type
To change one day and do right
Wake up one day ... and regret that you made it this way
But, probably not
That would take too much sense - that I know you ain't got
So, while I'm speaking on you, just this one time
With this one rhyme - I just have to say
Before, I ended the page
Thanks for never showing up at my house
With your bad vibe and your dark clouds
And again for this child - who does me proud ...
Of course, your thanks goes on this court decree
- which means nothing to me but

Deadbeat Poetry

I NEED YOU TO HOLD ME LOOSELY

I need you to hold me loosely
Your arms are starting to feel like a noose to me
because you holding on too ... tightly
& your calls are becoming a nuisance
honestly - Not that heart crashing thing that it used to be
Because, it happens so constantly
Until ...I feel like you playing tug of war with telephone lines
Trying to pull me over to your side
drag me into your frame of mind
When hardheaded me getting sucked in
- to whatever dream world you stuck in
Is on a long list of future things - that won't ever happen
& you're making all that a distraction
When all I need ... is for you to
..... Hold me loosely ...
I just need to be told I'm beautiful sometimes ...
And have things stroked & be touched, once and awhile
But, even my body language ... doesn't say forever
So, stop planning out how we gone be together
And how you gone move me to some state where I ain't ever wanted to be
- away from my family
So, we can buy a big house and live tax free
- Boy, you're crazy
You're so set on your plans to give me all the things
That I never wanted nor asked for - and don't need
That you can't see
that my focus ain't money and material things ...
pretty much ,all the things I love in life are free
And if you'd ever been listening to me
You'd know that the type of man I need to love me
Ain't got to have much really .... A nice physique
And a personality that's suited to me
... and he'll let me be the big spoon
So, I'll know that even when we're sleeping - he can still be depended on to
be held on to

- the kind of man that'll pray with me
While you don't take God seriously
I need the kind of man that - when we're up
We're going to be up together
When we're broke - we're gonna laugh & love
- until things get better
We're gonna sit in the dirt together and look up
hold hands & not give up -
- on anything ...
We're going to constantly get lost in each other's eyes
... and refuse to come back - right away ....
His kiss will take my breath away
And you don't make me feel any of those ways
So ... hold me loosely
& Quit talking about you want to marry me
How your mama keeps saying we were 'meant to be'
Because, she claims - she saw our wedding in a dream
Boy, you can't find a big enough ring
To bind me in a house with you
- and all the things I don't like - that you do
Seems like nothing gets through
when I try to tell you that you ain't the one for me
Instead of us suffocating in your emotions
- why can't you let me breathe & let us be ...
and just ...I need you to .... hold me loosely ....
I just want to have some laughs in your bed
Watch t.v. while I stroke your head
Talk to you ... when I need to de-stress
But, we ain't gone make it – unless ...
You hold me loosely ...

DEAR SIR

(A POEM ABOUT WHY MY BABY'S DADDYS PROBABLY CAN'T STAND ME)
Based on absolutely Real Facebook messages...
- I swear I couldn't make this stuff up -

* The more I try to finish this book, I swear the more it keeps writing itself.

I know I shouldn't do this, but I wrote it 'cause can't nobody else sound like that angry black woman that we baby's mamas become sometimes...

When a man - you may or may not have used to have loved - talks to you like he done lost his mind.

Don't appreciate how hard you be trying or he's the kind that won't give you anything but a free piece of his mind.

The baby's mamas who will read this true conversation and think they've been through this same type of conversation a few times.

Or probably been through baby daddy situations way worse than mine ....

This is ain't so much a poem - as it is part of my all true baby mama story - based on Facebook lines ...

THE BABY'S DADDY (whose name is left out to protect the innocent – not him of course, the innocent)

March 28 at 6:01am

T .T. I told I told you I needed to talk to you, and I want to talk to my daughter, please give me a call, or let here call me.

Sent via Facebook Mobile

T.T King April 3 at 1:21am

Dear Sir,

I'm updating the pics on my Facebook page, so you can see an updated version of your childs face, since you seem so agitated

 - though you don't know and can't spell her middle name and ain't never called her on a birthday.

And I passed along the message that you sent and the phone number, hopefully you old enough to not wonder

why she don't care to call.

And if you don't - let me just tell you that it's because it's so evident that you don't care at all.

But, I can't keep having the same conversations about it that's why I didn't write back at all ...

I just told her yesterday that she has your laugh and that dimple and she's hoping she'll be tall like you.

You're welcome to Facebook her a message any time and I promise I'll put it right through. I been out of this thing for a long time boy - **THE REST OF YOU AND HER IS UP TO YOU.**<-I put that shit in bold letters to make sure the words get through :)

I wrote you this poem off the top of my head cause it's all I could do ...

and you probably didn't even know it was a poem, because (boy) you ain't never got a clue **(lol) @you**

Now that you get it -

You'll probably write me one back that says (forget) you lol but, that's cool ... that's you.

Hopefully, you've grown up and will just start to hit her up and let her get to know you , the way your other kids do.

I swear on everything this is the last thing I'll probably ever say to you.

But like I said, ANY MESSAGE YOU WOULD LIKE TO SEND - I SWEAR I WILL SEND IT RIGHT THROUGH.   T.T. KING

April 3 at 10:09am Report

THE BABY'S DADDY : Yes and I guess your lil smart a** made all the right decisions in life, but she's growing up and you right it want have anything to do with you, it seems like your going to be a bitter person all your little life.

Sent via Facebook Mobile

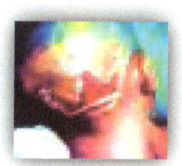

T.T. King April 4 at 1:09pm

Dang boy, that was a whole paragraph you could have written to her and for her. You're welcome to do so at any time -I PROMISE I'LL GET IT RIGHT TO HER .No matter what it says.

(* and etcetera ... I showed a lot of restraint not getting into the fact that I'm not bitter - I'm blessed, because I ain't got time for that boy and his mess ... notice there was a curse word thrown in there, on his part - but <u>not one</u> thank you. That's alright though, I'm still praying that God touch him.) - Update : Y'all I swear I wasn't going to print any more of our conversation. Then- I opened this:

THE BABY'S DADDY: Well you didn't accept me as a friend yet, do I could see them.

T.T. King April 7 at 3:28pm - (my response after re-adding him)
You're Welcome.

THE BABY'S DADDY April 7 at 3:39pm Report
Are you gone let here call me, or you gone give me your number miss king.
(Now to those of us, who can spell the word her (*and* won't ... and 'you're: plural for you are) did y'all not clearly read me tell that boy in bold letters to write her ? -That I did give her his number and the message? Why in the world would she want him to call her when he won't take time to get to know her & let her get to know him? More, than that, how does *he* not get that? And more importantly **- how is this boy thirty something years old and can't spell**? Anyway ... y'all see, he called me 'miss king' at the end. He was trying to be cute but, he got the idea from me so at least he learned something today. - So, in an effort to stay lady-like in this situation - I didn't respond to his last message and don't plan on doing so. Since, this book is like therapy , this is the message ***I wish*** I could have sent him back (but, I didn't -keep in mind I didn't **(:**

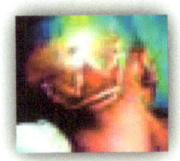

T.T. King (*The immature message that I wish the new me -would let the old me- in me send* **:)** EDITED

Dear Sir,

I told you I updated the (pictures) – and tried to be nice about it

Even though, I already knew you was gone act stupid- choose one word and try to start a fight about it

I even looked past your mis -typed attitude -and the general (uncool person) you've been

 and re-added (you) as my Facebook friend

Even though that's not even a category I can ever see us in, again...

& I did all these things expediently and benevolently

- so, I don't know what (else) you want from me

& NO - you cannot have my number - because I'm the one who pays the phone bill
And don't ever want the displeasure of hearing your voice on the other end ...
I'm just gone sit back and wait out this 'trying to communicate'-blue moon you're in ...
watch another one of your weak attempts to rebuild and re-burn the same bridge
... then walk over the ashes with your other kids
I Am Convinced that you are an Idiot. Period
So, I had her make her own page so she could discuss things herself with you
Because, I do not have the time or inclination to be trying keep dealing with you
I hope you accepted her friend request, cause with me (you are) re-unfriended and re-discontinued
and I'm re-blocking your messages as soon as I get back online
The woman in me, that believe in the Lord ,was just trying to give you some time
- to see her request and respond ...
I hope if I ever have to speak to you again ... He has re-calibrated your mind
... as well as mine
So, I could ever so I could ever share more than ten words with you - without wanting to slap (you) numerous times ....

(I can't close out this book without thanking him though because, he's one of the reasons I am what I am. So, thank you and thank God for you boy - we won't even discuss the fact that you misspelled the word her- Facebook ain't got spellcheck and Jesus loves you. - the moral of course being always - turn your little tragedies into triumphs and if we're lucky – misery into money.)

Walking In Mama's Shoes

I always knew that one day I would walk in mama's shoes
Do the same in front of the stove two step - to mama's same
'Lord bring us some more food 'blues
- whatever I didn't know in life, those shoes would walk me to the clues
I would put them on and my woman's' mind would know exactly what to do ...
I always knew that one day mama's shoes would fit my feet
That's why I watched her before I could speak
Learned how to do the 'back of the bra strap reach'
How to say, "Amen" - when the preacher preach
How to be strong but, yet meek
Kiss a man on da cheek and make his knees go weak ...
Because, when I contemplated mama's shoes - I could feel
that the magic was in the heels ....
I knew whenever I put those shoes on
I would understand the words to love songs
and sing along while I put my lipstick on
... about how that no good man done did me wrong ....
While I dabbed my neck with sweet cologne
And smoothed on lotion until my skin shone
Because, that's what I saw mama do
In her black slip and those shoes
so, I just knew
That those heels would be my body's exclamation points ...
they would accentuate the swivel of my hip joints
... and walk me through a few strange beds
just like even my mama's ,mama's ,mama's ... shoes did
I knew my mama's heels would strut me past the no good men
-to the one that was absolutely real
And I know that's the truth
That's why - I rock my shoes with beauty determination & attitude
Plus, I can still give the back of these heels two clicks - make a wish
and be back home again ....

All I have to do is call mama on the phone again
Let her voice remind the child in me that I'm not alone again
Get nourished by her wisdom then I'm on my own again
-So I shed some inner light on what I didn't do right
So, I don't get it wrong again
Press repeat on my stereo and play my song again
Figure out which way to point these heels, then baby it's on again
So, even though mama's shoes are still too big for my feet to fill
Like I said – now I got my
own heels
So, just like her I sling my babies around my hip
making corn bread and breast milk
& I make my own rules
& pay my own dues
While I'm walking in mama's shoes

DEDICATIONS

EVERYBODY KNOWS THAT I AM – CRAZY, BOSSY, ALWAYS WANT TO HAVE MY WAY AND HAVE NO SELF CONTROL-AND THE PEOPLE WHO REALLY KNOW ME KNOW THAT ALL THE GOOD I HAVE IN ME OUTWEIGHS ALL OF THAT. Thank God for all of my real 'peoples' that know and love all sides of me , and let me be me- TO ALL THE PEOPLE WHO BELIEVED IN ME- YOU KNOW I LOVE YOU BACK.

First and foremost, my baby's no matter how much bigger you get than me:

Trey and Kisura

THIS BOOK IS DEDICATED : To Trey -Boy, you laugh just like your daddy, and act just like me -and I still wonder where you get it from ... A perfect mixture of yo whole family tree but, of course , of 'Treys' there can only be one- my son .You hate my stuff so, probably will never read even this first dedication poem. Though this part specifically for you and everything we've been through ... While I'm standing here amazed at your break-through and the fact that I helped in creating you. You six feet tall to my 4"11 and in a few ways I look up to you. I don't do some of the things that I used to do – because of some knowledge you kicked even in your youth ... it's another poem in this book that will verify what I stand by– that one of the best parts of me is you. So, I'm proud of the man you're becoming though, I'll always see your baby face..Trey. And Kisura-whose name means beautiful - you know this is all dedicated to you too. The one so quiet, yet deep enough to swim through. Don't trip about the man who left you, mature enough to know it's not just about the journey we go through-but the people who take the time to walk with you... and you're the light we follow through your quiet sometimes. Hold your own part of a home down–the one that don't just notice the frown but, cares about it. Baby, you go through life so sweet and ain't complete unless you somewhere around me. They say can't nobody else get close to you because I keep you so close under my wing, but everybody smart - knows to stay close to beautiful things, I just happened to have one that was born to me ... And to mama - I don't mean to be redundant but, it all comes back to you -' cause I'm you in abundance. The root to my tree the one who keeps me grounded spiritually and hold me down in the seasons when all my leaves leave, them ones that blew away in the breeze. We fight once a year but that's just you and me ... because you the thing I'll always believe. Always wear dresses cause you old testament and know you have to separate yourself in order to lead ...You taught me greatness in independence and that prayer will get me through this thing and not to just have the faith of a mustard seed but, of the biggest oak in Yosemite. And to my dad - jack of all trades and lingual master of everything - the best absent father that God had for me ... always a phone call away so it's like you stayed with me - and made sure you didn't get off the phone until I was sure I knew everything ... IN THE WORLD . A card every September for 35 years , though I've only seen your face a few times but, your voice has wiped away my tears and toughened me up from my fears so many times....You are that constant voice that the girl in me will always need ..and the woman in me will always heed.. and thank you because the wisest parts of me- came from you. I get this artistic thing from you too, so you know what it means to me. When I look back through our history ,it came to me that I was meant to be.. you're what every father who can't be there physically should strive to be ... .(TO MY READERS CHECK OUT MY DAD'S ART ONLINE Sometime - JAHN BRONSON - HE'S AMAZING) .And of course, this dedication is to **Angie** when everybody else run -you stand with me. My best friend who always understand -when don't nobody else get me .'Told me "Girl, just come home.", when I was defeated-and my own family didn't give a damn about nothing I needed - didn't care that I was beat down ,broke down and f'd up - couldn't bother to be tainted with my bad luck. - You Angie –you- that old Cancer girl with that true, stick like glue - kind of love - dug them claws in me and ain't never gave up .... on me or my dreams ...The only person who ever read <u>everything</u> I ever wrote .... Know enough to know that right now you're choked up because you know my ode to you is some of the realest s*** I ever wrote.. We got that stuff can't nobody else join in cause when we met somehow we was born in ... the reason I'm immortalizing our friendship in pen .I re-did these dedications because my first draft didn't say enough about you ... and all the people that I love-: Jossy, Jayden & Xavier aunt T.T. put you in a verse so you can say your name was in a book that got the world shook ... and you saw me writing it in the living room – so you always know that your circumstances can never contain you ... and all of you are so beautiful ...To Marie & Nanna Pie (see..y'all readers don't know chasing me left me wandering aimlessly a few times) & to Lawrence the sweetest, most hustling'ist man I know, whenever I needed to be somewhere you was ready to go , pawned ya xbox so I could have money for the bus and for some reason just chose to love us...which is why we will always love you ... to my big headed 'nephew' Chris Washington (you know I love you boy). To Aunt Betty who let me read her books and to ALL of my Grandma's - and to HAMPTON streets because, what would a T.T. King be- if it wasn't for y'all? And to my first love J.Stokes for teaching me the meaning of: "The same thing that will make you laugh will make you cry ...", but thank God - if we're lucky those are some of the best belly laughs of your life. And to my brother Chris King - I know you had to leave so that you could get your wings - recognize my soul and know me by my new name when I see you again. Thank you for everything …. You are one of the most important things in my history and what I am presently…. (I can't put that in the past tense because I can feel your spirit around me). And a 'what's up wit 'cha to my sisters - Shelette, Detra, Dana and Licia .And first in my heart – <u>THIS BOOK IS DEDICATED TO GOD</u> . My lips were formed just to praise you, my life just to love you and my testimony to exalt you … and to any human persons I may have I forgot, charge that to my head but, definitely not to my heart. And to my fans this book is dedicated to you … I love you too, though we just met ….. (To my poetic heroes: Dana Gilmore, Georgia Me and Inyanla Vanzant - the poem "<u>Today I Smiled</u>", is a tribute to her "<u>Yesterday I Cried</u>" poem and Langston Hughes, who was eloquent yet simple .To Usher and Jazmin Sullivan for the lyrics and to all the talented graphic artists I found online for their interpretation of beauty and expression.) .

I hope y'all enjoyed me as much as I loved sharing myself with you. Please keep reading with me. Slangetry II is on the way, along with my book of short stories , and a full-length fiction novel that I can't wait for y'all to read. If any of these poems touch you feel free to drop me a line on www.slangetry .com -all poets are welcome to drop some lyrics in the 'Slangetry Spot' on my page.

A short Slang* glossary:

TERMS - *Ain't – am/are not
*Cha' – you
*I'mo – I am going to
Wanna – want to
Y'all – you all
*Yo' – your

DEFINITIONS:

* Baby-mama-ology - knowledge that smart women always try to impart even and especially to their slowest 'baby's daddies'

*Blue boyz – police officers

* Deadbeat – parent that doesn't support their children, either monetarily or emotionally (i.e. dodging child support letters, getting paid under the table or illegitimate money in order to negate financial responsibility to their offspring

*Downlow – 1. The act of perpetrating the outward persona of heterosexuality while secretly having sexual relations with persons of the same sex 2. the act of committing a negative or underhanded act

*Dred – singular slang term for dreadlocks- a hairstyle where natural hair is twisted into long matted or ropelike locks.

*Game – 1. A series of patterned 'rules' perpetuated by a person in order to 'win'- by following said rules to gain a desired result 2. Convincing someone to bend to ones will and act outside of their natural character or state of being, by manipulating the brain and/or emotions.

*Hit - A person whose sole purpose is to have physical relations with, with little other contact other than sex /or in between physical liaisons

*Ho-etry - The act of committing a constant series of whore-like actions (i.e. sleeping with a lot of different sexual partners, usually within a very short period of time)

*Feds – Federal Police Agents

*Lame – Person whose personality or standards not up to an acceptable social level

*Spit - To speak from the heart about a subject of vast importance

*Spooning - Sleeping position in which participants sleep with one holding the other in the chest to back position, usually with all points touching from shoulders to feet.

* Swagger - Confidence; Self-possessed walk reinforced by material possessions (i.e. nice clothes, car etc.)

*The Big Spoon - The person holding the sleeper in the spooning position.

*Tims - Short for timberland boots

*Tracks - Culmination line of hair in which false extensions are attached to scalp for lengthening, thickening fine hair etc.

*Weave - False hair extensions, either real (grown from human) or synthetic (made from materials)

*Whips – Cars ; Automobiles

www.ingramcontent.com/pod-product-compliance
Lightning Source LLC
Chambersburg PA
CBHW040026050426
42453CB00002B/21